English Lantern Clocks

English Lantern Clocks

W. F. J. Hana

Translated by
E. J. Tyler

BLANDFORD PRESS
Poole   Dorset

First published in the U.K. in 1979

English text copyright
© 1979 Blandford Press Ltd
Link House, West Street, Poole,
Dorset, BH15 ILL

British Library Cataloguing in Publication Data

Hana, W F J
English lantern clocks.
1. Clocks and watches – England – Collectors
and collecting
I. Title II. Tyler, Eric John
739.3   NK7495.G7

ISBN 0 7137 1011 X

Originally published in the
Netherlands as *Engelse
Lantaarnklokken*

World copyright © 1977 Unieboek b.v.,
Bussum

Set in 11/13pt Century Schoolbook
and printed in Great Britain by BAS
Printers Limited, Over Wallop,
Hampshire

Bound by Robert Hartnoll Ltd,
Bodmin, Cornwall

Contents

*Dedicated with respect to the memory of
my friend A. W. Pelckmans, who first
guided my footsteps along the path to
discovering antique clocks.*

W.F.J.H.

Acknowledgements

The following photographs are Crown copyright and are reproduced by courtesy of the Science Museum, London: Plates 1, 2, 3.

We are also grateful for permission to reproduce clocks from the following collections:—
Bijl Collection, Schiedam, Netherlands: Plates 18, 40, 47, 57, 59, 85, 112.
Kats Collection, Rotterdam: Plates 28, 52, 94, 95, 114, 115.
Stender, St Michielsgestel—Holland: Plate 107.

Documentation, implying that a certain dealer or collector once possessed a particular clock but now has only the photograph and information, has been kindly provided by the following:—
Geerd Wijnen, Amsterdam: Plates 8, 63, 64, 71, 81, 86, 87, 96.
F. Kats, Rotterdam: Plates 10, 11, 15, 23, 29, 53, 61, 66, 76.
Stender, St Michielsgestel—Holland: Plates 12, 14, 17, 19, 20, 21, 22, 26, 27, 30, 31, 32, 33, 37, 43, 44, 45, 46, 48, 49, 58, 60, 62, 65, 67c, 69, 70, 84, 92, 99, 101.
Gerald Marsh, Winchester, England: Plates 39, 42, 55, 56, 93.
H. Kreft, Rotterdam: Plates 51, 89, 90.
Ronald A. Lee, London: Plate 107.

Preface

Collecting antiques has enjoyed a tremendous boom since World War 2.

The result has been that prices of antiques of good quality have continually risen. Naturally, the quantity available of original pieces can never be increased for the very simple reason that one cannot create genuine antique objects. By definition an antique piece has been around for a long time, often a very long time, and it is this passage of time that cannot be reproduced. However, it is only too obvious that many craftsmen, and often clever ones at that, try to do just this. One only has to look at the many imitations that are offered for sale to see what is going on. Often the dealer concerned is 'in the know', but sometimes where extremely clever fakes are being dealt with, he is completely unsuspecting.

Antiques of all types are being discovered daily, while other pieces are coming on to the market as a result of being sold by private individuals. It also happens that people who are attracted by the high prices of antiques dispose of family heirlooms, but antiques also come onto the market from the estates of deceased collectors. Luckily, not every important collection is handed over to the trustees or given to a museum so that nothing is offered for sale after the death of the owner. I say 'luckily' because when important pieces appear on the market, today's collectors are given an opportunity to enlarge their collection—and without the trade in antiques, one would never be able to acquire a collection!

What I have said about antiques in general applies in particular to that small part of the antique world which is the topic of this book—the English lantern clock and its variations.

Previous publications make it apparent that most enthusiasts enjoy looking at pictures. In order to be able to compare pieces accurately it is necessary to see them, and it is a fact that a good photo can tell more than many pages of text. This may sound like a truism. However when technical matters are being explained in words, there is always the disadvantage that it is difficult to make clear to non technically minded people just how things are arranged and how they work. An illustration can solve this problem very simply, but when I have found such an explanation unavoidable, I have kept it as short and as clear as possible.

It is hoped that this book, which does indeed include a good number of photographs of lantern clocks, will do justice to a type of clock that has a special interest for collectors and dealers.

As far as possible and where the information is available, the year of birth and death of the clockmaker concerned has been included in the caption to each illustration; or sometimes I have given the period when he was a member of the Clockmakers' Company. This has been done in the same manner that Baillie used in his indispensable book *Watchmakers and Clockmakers of the World*.

'CC' means member of the Clockmakers' Company with the relevant years, 'mCC' means Master of the Clockmakers' Company, 'a' means apprenticed which means that the maker was apprenticed to the master who is mentioned.

*   *   *

I would like to end by expressing my sincere thanks to the various people connected with the trade who have put indispensable material at my disposal or have given me the opportunity to photograph lantern clocks from their collections.

In particular, Mr F. Kats of Rotterdam provided important documentation and at the same time gave constructive criticism. Mr E. Stender of St Michielsgestel provided many excellent photographs. I also received some equally excellent photographs from Mr Geerd Wijnen of Amsterdam and Mr Kreft of Rotterdam, while Mr S. Bijl of Schiedam gave me the chance to photograph many different clocks. For the clock in the especially fine colour photograph on the cover, I am indebted to Mr Meyrick Neilson of Tetbury. Mr Gerald Marsh of Winchester gave me some splendid photographs, as also did the British Museum (Science), through the good offices of Mr R. J. Law.

Finally, I would not like to forget all the other collectors who allowed their clocks to be photographed. For obvious reasons they must remain anonymous, but their help is of great importance and very much appreciated. Indeed, I thank most heartily all these good horological friends, dealers and amateurs. I need hardly add that spontaneous help like this is indispensable in a work of this kind.

W.F.J.H.
Ulvenhout, Netherlands

1 Collecting Antique Clocks

Every calling is a conspiracy

George Bernard Shaw

I will begin the first chapter of this clock book with the question that is so often posed, 'How do you get hold of these clocks?' Well, the answer seems simple—by buying them. But it is not as simple as all that. The next question usually asked is 'Where can you buy them?' To this comes an answer that opens up many different possibilities: 'From the antique trade'. Of course, sometimes it is also possible to buy from a private owner, but this does not often happen.

The Antique Trade

On examination, the antique trade resolves itself into a number of specialists; for instance the dealer who apparently has his shop full of everything, but can still have his particular preferences. Next to him we find the real specialist who does business almost exclusively in one particular line. One thinks here of paintings, porcelain, silver, pewter and bronze objects, furniture and carpets, to name but a few specialities. There are also specialists who occupy themselves exclusively with antique clocks. This part of the trade embraces not only antique clocks and watches themselves, but also antiques having some sort of connection with the subject. Indeed, in this section of the trade we sometimes find sundials, astrolabes and other measuring instruments, while some other dealers may also have musical boxes and barometers in stock. Certain individuals complete this by dealing in antique books on subjects in their area, although strictly speaking here we are in the territory of the secondhand and antiquarian bookseller.

Although the number of *bona fide* specialists in most countries is small, the antique trade is international. It is quite normal for many dealers to travel abroad widely, adding to their collections—or at least trying to do so. At the present time it is more difficult to buy good quality antiques than it is to sell them. The collector who knows the ropes often buys from dealers overseas; after all, modern communications are so good that this aspect no longer gives rise to any problems.

In general, it is fair to say that a large number of antiques are purchased with an eye to investment. Clocks take an important place here because as well as their purely monetary value, they enhance the appearance of the home.

There is a brisk European trade in antique clocks, especially between the Netherlands, Britain and France, with a trend in recent years for many clocks to be sold from Germany and Austria. And strange as this may seem, trade with USA is bringing many clocks back to Europe. These items are clocks which were taken out from Europe centuries ago by emigrants—and now they are starting to come back.

Many groups of dealers organise Antique Fairs. There are now a good many each year and one can often purchase very fine clocks at such fairs, whether local or national. The dealers concerned guarantee the authenticity and perfect working order of their clocks in many cases. Antique fairs, or more correctly exhibitions of things that can be sold, are very popular and often the best pieces are sold on the opening day. Overseas dealers often buy here and the specialised collector is a certain attender.

The smaller fairs have sprung up like mushrooms in the last few years. The smaller traders were naturally lured on by the continued success of the large fairs, whereupon they organised something of the same sort. Alas, it must be confessed that many of the small fairs do not offer what the purchaser expects to find. The idea that one can get hold of good quality clocks for a song is untrue. If something good does turn up then a fantastic price is asked, while generally no guarantee of authenticity or good working order will be given. As a result, the real experts can buy what they like at the small fairs because they can see what they are buying and easily judge just what condition a piece is in. Let the layman be warned and not buy without the vital (preferably written) guarantee.

It is a sad fact that there are still antique fairs where one can find downright rubbish at fancy prices. Apparently these dealers seem unable to see they are making a laughing stock both of themselves and the trade.

Societies and Publications

In order to acquire the addresses of dealers and collectors, it is most advisable to join a good society of lovers of antique clocks. Perhaps the best know is the Antiquarian Horological Society, usually known as AHS. Though based in England, this internationally slanted society has a membership of a thousand or so over the whole world. Meetings are regularly held in London, but the important feature for overseas members is that an excellent quarterly journal is published. It is a treasure house of relevant information and provides good contacts between collectors of similar interests as well as very good information. Questions and answers are published regularly and there are interesting small advertisements and book reviews, and the horological antique trade advertises in grand style. In addition each AHS member receives from time to time a complete list of members in the form of a neatly printed book. That this is a priceless source of information goes without saying.

In Germany there is the Freunde Alter Uhren. This society has fewer overseas members but publishes a well documented book each year called *Schriften der Freunde Alter Uhren* in which there are articles and advertisements. The French also have a thriving Society and there are others, particularly in the USA. Membership of these societies is no costly matter and is certainly worthwhile if only to receive the regular publications.

There are of course other publications on clocks outside those of the horological societies and it is also advisable to look at the magazines published in the general field of antiques, for there may often be something of interest to the clock collector.

Buying a Clock

Assuming that you are a complete beginner, but have an interest in antique clocks, you are still awaiting an answer to the question posed at the beginning of this chapter 'How do we get hold of antique clocks?'

Naturally, you can always go into an antique shop without any preliminaries. Under favourable circumstances you may meet a reputable dealer; but it can also happen that you come up against an out-and-out swindler. In which case on your own head be it (and on your money), for according to Dr de Jong,* a swindler is 'acute, fluent, domineering and unprincipled.'

Although Dr de Jong is describing the political swindler in this case, his striking character study also fits the swindler in antiques. In case of any doubt or lack of knowledge, always ask for advice before you buy. It is one of those oddities of life that so often one comes across an expert *after* one has purchased (and paid). Therefore ask for advice beforehand; it can save you a lot of unpleasantness. Do not have your hand forced, for disreputable dealers have a habit of saying 'You must

---

*Dr L. de Jong *Het Koninkrijk der Nederlanden in de tweede wereldoorlog.* 4 1. helft blz 415.

choose tonight because I have another keen customer coming back in the morning.' Sometimes this customer really exists, but more often he does not and is only brought in to being so as to make you give a quick decision. This sort of dealer thinks that business is more interesting with this kind of tale, but it has the reverse effect on the cautious customer.

If you are not an expert, ask the dealer, whether he allows expert examination. If he is *bona fide* and sells objects of quality he will always allow it. If the whole affair is not above board, it is then that the evasive chatter starts. In short: think before you buy and don't be carried away by the excitement of the moment. It is clear that if you are knowledgeable yourself, you can buy safely everywhere: if you are not, get advice from experts who are well known.

This advice also holds good for auctions. There are excellent auctions and auctioneers who are extremely trustworthy—but there are, alas, others. Do not rely entirely on descriptions made in good faith in the catalogues. Attend the preview before you buy. There are actually sales where 'The Trade' have their doubtful pieces sold so that their otherwise good reputation does not suffer. It may also happen that you see a certain clock moving from sale to sale; you keep seeing it again and again. Make your decision: keep off it. This is not the place to go into certain unsavoury practices that take place at some auctions, but it is vital that you keep a sharp lookout wherever you go.

Buying from private individuals is not simple either. Many people who want to sell a clock believe that they are dealing in solid gold. It is the first rule of the game never to give them your opinion; let the seller do all the talking. Never be enthusiastic, for that immediately influences the price. Let the vendor think what he likes about his clock. If you make him (or her) wiser than he was, then he either becomes more expensive or angry. It often happens that people offer something which they really think is rare, but which in fact is nothing out of the ordinary. In these cases, if you draw the vendor's attention to the real facts, then the fur really starts to fly!

Look out also for vendors who advertise. In advertisements they often promise you a cow with a golden horn, while the real joke is that good clocks never need to be advertised. In fact purchasers can *always* be found for a good piece. Naturally, the advertisements of reputable dealers in trade papers do not come under this heading, and I am thinking only of the small 'ads' in the columns of the national dailies. The descriptions of the clocks that one sees in these columns speak volumes; French pendulum clocks, Cockerel clocks, Harp pendulum clocks, Flower pendulum clocks—and all this means is 'Comtoise', the French clocks from the Comté that were almost always kept in cases and of which the loose movements are now being sold.

In these columns you also find the announcements of the small antique fairs. Certainly it can be interesting to visit such a fair, but do not expect to find bargains. In fact there is really no one in trade circles that does not know this. One can sometimes buy something good abroad for a reasonable price, but then the vendor is usually very knowledgeable on the highest price he can ask.

Antique Clock Collections

The novice collector will probably ask where he can see a good collection of clocks. This brings us to the museums, for private collectors do not usually display their collections to the public.

In England there are outstanding collections to be seen, such as in the British Museum and the Science Museum in London, while in Oxford is the important Museum of the History of Science. In Paris is the Conservatoire Nationale des Arts et Métiers and the Musée des Beaux Arts.

In the Netherlands are the Rijksmuseum in Amsterdam, City Museum at The Hague, The Boymans-van Beuningen Museum at Rotterdam and the Museum of Science at Leiden.

In Germany and Austria there are also a number of interesting museums for the clock lover: at Kassel the Hessisches Landesmuseum, at Furtwangen the museum of the School for Precision Engineering and there are also clocks in the Bayerisches National Museum in Munich, while the collections of the Württembergisches Landesmuseum and the Landesgewerbeamts Baden-Württemberg in Stuttgart are also interesting. In Vienna are the collections in the Kunsthistorisches Museum while the Vienna clock museum is also of interest.

In Switzerland you can find the museum of horology at La Chaux de Fonds while there is also a museum of horology at Le Locle. In Winterthur we find the famous Kellenberger collection. This collection includes many fine late Gothic examples including those by members of the Liechti family.

Collecting and Collectors

At first sight one finds the same characteristics among collectors of old clocks as among, for example, collectors of postage stamps. Some collect everything they can get, others exclusively English antique clocks and others only table clocks, wall clocks or long case clocks. Also, in the clock world, there are collectors of certain styles or periods, while there are technically minded people who collect as many different types of movement as possible. The group you belong to or want to belong to is not so important, provided that you always bear in mind that only quality can benefit your collection. Quality work can always be sold again, but one is stuck with rubbish.

Investors have also turned their eyes towards antique clocks in recent years. When an investor buys a clock, he is doing something understandable quite independently of whether he wants it to decorate his home. Investors have also been known to take the clock straight to the vault of their bank. In such cases, there is then only the pleasure of possession and none of the beauty, which to many people comes first.

Whether you possess few or many clocks, it is always advisable to photograph or have photographed the valuable objects that you possess. Alas, thefts of antiques, including clocks, are a feature of modern life, so with an eye on the insurance it is important that you should be able to show what has disappeared. If your collection is large, it is only common sense to have a valuation made. In connection with insurance a good description with sharp photos can protect you from great financial damage in serious cases.

Think of it this way. An insurance company will accept one or a few valuable clocks as part of the household effects. If your clocks clearly form a collection, then the matter is somewhat different. I stress this— and your author is *not* employed in the insurance business—take out a special insurance for your collection. Admittedly in the case of a robbery you do not usually get your clocks back, but it is worse if not only your clocks but your invested money has gone too.

If your collection is very valuable, the insurance company may require an alarm system to reduce the risk of break-ins. Such an installation, provided it is of good quality, is above all a source of comfort.

Restoration Work

The condition in which one can find antique clocks varies from perfect to pitiful. No comment is needed on the first instance, but as soon as a clock cannot be called perfect, we have to go into the question of what has to be done to bring such a piece into a state of perfection.

In most cases, clocks offered for sale need repairs and sometimes also require restoration. The expert dealers with good reputations deliver clocks in a perfect state, otherwise the trouble is upon their own heads, sometimes literally. If a clock is purchased in a damaged condition, where the vendor cannot arrange for repair, then we have to see whether the necessary work is simple or complicated. Unfortunately, the number of repairers and restorers who can do perfect work is very small. That is just the beginning of the difficulties for those who are not at home in a specialist field and thus do not know which way to proceed next.

As a result of the small number of good repairers, it is natural that these people are much in demand and it is normal for them to have waiting lists; unfortunately this takes some of the pleasure away. Certainly there are better possibilities for repair in England than most other countries, but the difficulty still exists. It remains unthinkable to have a non-perfect repair which makes the clock go again but does nothing else to it. Thus it is hard to understand why there are so few experienced younger clock repairers. The training of the technical schools concentrates more on replacing spare parts and cleaning watches than on real handwork. The present day tendency to throw away something that is broken and get a new one is a sad fact of consumer society. The tutors are not to blame any more than we can take the young horologists to task because they are not like their colleagues of fifty years ago. Handwork is not paid for; therefore no one does it any more. This does not help the owner of antique clocks for the repair of an antique implies 100% handwork. There are no spare parts, and if parts are lost or irreparably worn, they have to be made by hand out of good quality material. It is clear that this requires great skill, as well as costing a lot of time and therefore a lot of money. The discerning collector will not grumble about thorough restoration and repair, but he will complain about work that is done in record time and leaves its traces behind.

The consequences are that properly carried out, and therefore long lasting, repairs can be costly. This should be realised at time of purchase. It should also mean that the horological educational authorities should pause to think about clocks which are called antique even if training were only optional. It can be guaranteed that a good craftsman who devotes himself to antique work can earn a good income. This naturally requires experience and initiative from the candidate. The experience can be obtained from the existing repairers; the love of fine handwork has to be part of the students personality and philosophy.

2 English Lantern Clocks

What is understood remains. What is badly learnt is forgotten.
Professor Dr J. Jongbloed

The English lantern clock, also called 'Bedpost' or 'Birdcage', came into existence about 1600 and was based on earlier types of wall clock. This makes us think of the Continent and then directly, for example, of the wall clocks which were made in Germany by members of the Liechti family of Winterthur in the second half of the 16th century, or of late 16th century South German wall clocks which should be considered the forerunners of the lantern clock.

It can be accepted that the earliest makers of lantern clocks, who were probably English, had seen these clocks or in some way had come into contact with them. This is suggested by the fact that the earliest English lantern clocks were made almost entirely of iron. These clocks always have striking mechanism. A good example of this is to be found in the British Museum (Science) in London, where an iron lantern clock is shown which is engraved with the words 'John Holloway att Lavington fecit 1611'. Only the chapter ring of this clock is of brass.

Brass is an alloy of copper and zinc (see also page 38). It is yellow in colour and considerably harder than the soft red copper. Copper itself is scarcely used in horology and when we do find it, it is always for non-working parts (on Austrian clocks we often find, for example, chapter rings made of silvered copper).

The actual date of the first lantern clock is not known. Sometime about 1600 is probable, for we know of many lantern clocks in the pre-pendulum period; the earliest examples have a verge escapement with a large wheel-balance as regulator. This wheel (Plate 4), is fastened to the verge, and is not as in later watches (1674) controlled by a balance spring. The slow tick which these clocks possess is the result of the size of the wheel, while the speed of running is determined by the size of the driving weight and the amplitude and moment of inertia of the balance. Thus the result that these clocks achieve as timekeepers is, according to modern

[17]

standards, very bad. They vary a great deal and are certainly not suitable for service as a domestic timekeeper. But then our requirements in the realm of exact timekeeping are somewhat different from those in the first half of the 17th century. The smallest unit then was a quarter-of-an-hour. As a result of this, lantern clocks from this period have only one hand, and the inner edge of the chapter ring is divided into quarter-hours. For that matter, these clocks were the only weight driven domestic clocks in use in England in the first half of the 17th century.

Such early clocks, provided they are in good condition, have become especially treasured collectors' pieces. Examples which have not been rebuilt later to a more modern system (verge escapement with short pendulum or even anchor escapement with long pendulum) are very rare and fetch high prices.

By rebuilding to pendulum, the whole rear plate with the alarm work was usually thrown away on account of the limited space. This is a somewhat rigorous intervention. The six main parts thrown away were:

1. The rear plate generally made of iron on which was mounted the alarm scapewheel with its sprocket, the spectacle shaped cord guide, and the cock for the alarm verge with hammer;
2. The alarm verge on which was mounted the hammer;
3. The complete alarm lifting piece which was supported between the dial, mostly above the XI, and the rear plate;
4. The flat spring with the release pin which was placed in the motion work over the hand arbor;
5. The beautifully engraved alarm setting disc; a part of the clock which to our taste is essential and forms a feature of the dial and therefore of the appearance of the clock;
6. The wire springs on the top plate between which the alarm verge moves.

There are still dealers, who on being told that the alarm work is missing say 'So you find it a disadvantage. Nobody else uses anything like that any more'.

There is an answer to this weak argument: if a clock originally had an alarm, the alarm belongs to it according to our way of thinking. It should work too, whether we use it or not. The lack of the alarm is a serious fault in the function and the outward appearance of the lantern clock.

It so happens that lantern clocks that were rebuilt in the late 17th and the 18th century are now being converted to their original condition. Naturally one can protest, but good restoration to the original form appears more attractive than a clock which does not possess its original escapement. Of course this work needs to be done with the utmost skill. Alas, much butchery is discovered in this connection, but that also applies to the entire field of restoring antiques. I find it incomprehensible that there are people who maintain that the value of an antique goes up through inexpert restoration and repair. It must be stressed that the opposite is the case. Rebuilding to escapements that give more exact results has been achieved in earlier centuries without worrying about it, and that is understandable. People had an object for use, and a very expensive one at that, and they tried to get the maximum utility from it. No one thought about destroying original work. We must see the early 17th century house clock as it was; an object of use for the fortunate individual. It is clear that with the advance in technique, people brought their possessions into line. And although this sounds stupid, we must be grateful to the 17th century owners of lantern clocks that they did have them rebuilt. Luckily they did not live in the throw away era that we in the 20th century have to endure. They made their clocks conform to the latest discoveries, with the result that we can possess them today. Even the rebuilding of a current model is no longer possible and certainly not economically justifiable: we throw it away and buy a new one. Through the enormous strides that technology has made, we now possess almost faultless quartz clocks, but are they really clocks any more? They are little computers with an ugly man-in-the-moon exterior. How unlike the difficulties of a lantern clock with a rebuilt escapement. The experienced restorer can see by empty holes and damage in the plates how the clock must have originally looked and restore the appearance.

Thus we first see lantern clocks as an English product, but the French were not idle in this field. Also the Italians made especially fine lantern clocks, but these are scarce and rarely come on to the market.

English lantern clocks can be regularly found with the better dealers. The lantern is now a very much appreciated clock being of reasonable dimensions and a wall clock that comes in various styles and takes up little room. The brass exterior is generally attractive. The production of English lantern clocks must have been fairly large on account of the regularity with which they appear. This type of clock though used everywhere in England, was gradually displaced in the second half of the 18th century by the long case clock that was derived from it. This is a development which took many decades. The lantern clock hanging on the wall had exposed weights and lines. To protect these (possibly from excitedly playing children) a metal rack was placed round them. A pleasanter method of protecting lantern clocks is seen in the rare 'Hooded Clocks'. These clocks have a simple but graceful case consisting of a seat on which the movement stands, covered by a removable hood with a door. One step further and it was placed in a long narrow case— and the long case clock was born. The dial changed to a square shape while the case followed the styles of the 18th century English furniture.

While the earliest long case clocks had a lantern movement with a

[19]

square dial, when the movement became hidden from sight it was also altered. The characteristic lantern type was no longer made and was replaced by one with two brass plates.

Constructional Mechanisms

The English lantern clock has a sturdy frame which consists of four turned columns between which the top and bottom plates are fastened. In most cases, these plates are fixed by the feet with the finials being screwed into the columns. It can also happen that the column together with the foot and finial is turned out of one piece. The plates are then slid into grooves and fastened with a stiff pin (Fig. 1). The arbors and wheels run between cross-shaped supports. The going train on balance clocks has three wheels; the Main wheel, the Second wheel and the Scapewheel. If a somewhat later clock has a verge escapement and short pendulum, then there are four wheels in the going train; Main wheel, Second wheel, Crown wheel and, above the top plate, horizontal Scapewheel. In this connection it ought to be mentioned that the clock with three wheels in the going train, the Balance clock, has a duration of about twelve hours, while the clock with four wheels can run for about thirty hours. This is true if the clock is not hung too low. The later lantern clocks with anchor escapement and long pendulum, which sometimes have three wheels in the going train, run somewhat longer than their predecessors with three wheels and a balance. This is, however, a result of the totally changed situation in the escapement and the provision of a longer pendulum.

The striking work placed behind the going train consists of a Great wheel, which is provided with the striking pins, the Hoop wheel, the Warning wheel and the Fly. The striking mechanisms of lantern clocks have a Count Wheel that is placed on the outside of the rear support and therefore they do not repeat. To put it simply: these clocks get out of step. There is, however, an important difference between the striking mechanism of lantern clocks and say that of the Dutch types. The lantern clock has a striking mechanism provided with 'warning' which means that the instant that striking begins is more carefully controlled than on clocks where the striking is released by the raising of a lever with a hinged nose controlled by a spring. This somewhat technical fact arises from the striking with warning being released in two operations. Some time before the hour, the striking mechanism begins to operate and one hears the wheels immediately brought to a halt without the clock striking. Precisely on the hour, the lifting piece falls, whereupon the clock strikes. It is certainly remarkable that such a perfect system is found in such early clocks and it is a fact that many more recently made clocks are provided with the less precise method using the hinged nose.

[20]

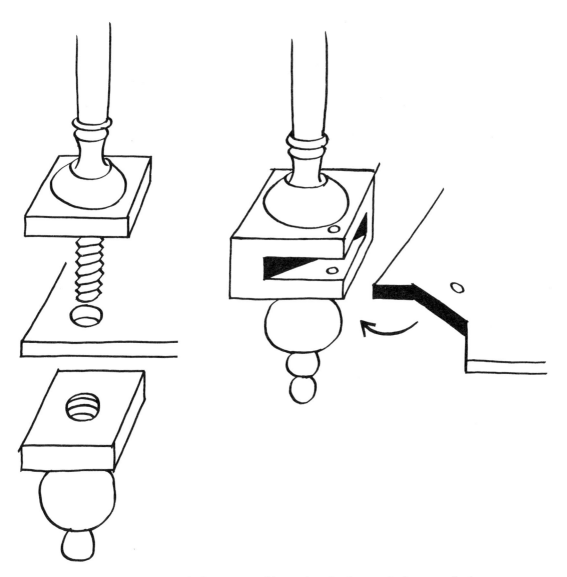

Fig. 1   The conventional English manner of fastening the frame of a lantern clock (left); however, the French method (right) is seen on some English lanterns.

The sprockets on the main arbors of both trains are furnished with spikes on the early movements to accomodate rope. When the spikes are sharp there is no problem with the rope slipping. An important disadvantage of the rope system is that the rope wears quickly and must be frequently renewed, while the clock becomes full of dust from the worn rope. This is worst on the bottom plate and on a very dusty clock the pivots run dry because the dust absorbs the oil. Cleaning is the only remedy, while afterwards fresh oil of good quality must be applied in the proper places. Because of this disadvantage, one sees many lantern clocks provided with sprockets for chains. These sprockets require an iron chain of the type that is seen made of brass in Black Forest clocks among others. It is thus downright wrong to use a 'Figure of eight' Frisian chain in a lantern clock. A recent development that is very useful is to fit coloured nylon rope. While it may clash with our aesthetic feelings to fit such a modern material in an antique clock, one must admit that the functioning of this rope is excellent. It does not get fluffy and form dust and it scarcely wears away and is very strong. Another advantage is that fixing hooks on this type of rope is very easy. The ends of the rope are melted on to the hooks by means of a heated screwdriver. It then seems advisable to use this type of rope purely in one's own interest, and all the more so in that it does the clock no harm.

The lantern clocks pre-dating about 1660, which means balance clocks, were driven by two lead weights, one for each train. The ropes were naturally held straight by two small counterpoises.

The weight for the going train always hangs on the left (as we stand in front of the dial) and the weight for the striking train on the right. This results in the main wheel for the going train turning anti-clockwise, while that for the striking train turns clockwise. This clockwise turning of the striking train implies that the hammer must be placed on the right. The pins in the great wheel push the hammer tail downwards, whereby the hammer is brought towards the centre of the clock. As the hammer tail escapes from a pin the hammer springs back to its original position by the pressure of a stiff steel spring and hits the bell.

On lantern clocks made after 1660, we find both trains (going and striking) driven by one weight with the well known pulley and counterpoise on the system of Christiaan Huygens. The pulleys used for lantern clocks are, however, of wood; the counterpoise is a fairly heavy lead ring, or better still, a small weight hung from a pulley. The result of driving by one weight is that the main wheels of both trains turn anti-clockwise with the direct result that the hammer is placed on the left hand side of the clock. As well as this, only the sprocket on the striking train is fitted with clickwork, while the early balance clock with two weights needed clickwork on both sprockets. The lead weights of the balance clock are, in fact, cylindrical buckets with a rounded bottom which are only partly filled with lead. As already mentioned, the force of the weight on these early clocks has an effect on the rate of going, so one starts with a weight that is too light and adds extra pieces of lead. These weights which are scarcely ever found in their original form, hang just like a real bucket, with a handle from an iron wire that is fastened to the outside of the weight.

Sometimes we find lantern clocks which have eight holes in the bottom plate; four large holes to allow the rope from the sprockets to pass through together with two somewhat smaller ones on each side next to the doors (Plate 68). These holes are for holding the outer ends of the ropes with a knot and the going and the striking side each has to be provided with a pulley for the weight. This gives 100% increase in the time of running. This applies particularly to the balance clocks with a twelve-hour period. Naturally, the driving weight has to be 100% greater. The disadvantage is that too much weight has to be supported by the frame and it gets pulled out of shape.

The alarm work has already been mentioned. We now have to deal with the dial work. This is mounted on the front of the foremost support. On one-handed clocks, we find a pinion on the extended arbor of the main wheel that drives a wheel placed above it. This wheel, the hour wheel, carries the hour hand on its arbor. If the clock has two hands, the extension of the main arbor is filed square and carries the minute wheel. This wheel drives the cannon pinion and thus the long hand while its pinion drives the hour wheel with the short hand.

On single handed clocks, we find a star with twelve points behind the hour wheel. This releases the striking. If the clock has two hands, this is achieved by a pin on the cannon pinion. If the clock has an alarm, there is a plate over the hour wheel pipe with a pin for releasing the alarm. The alarm setting disc is mounted on the pipe of this plate and stands in front of the dial.

The lifting pieces for locking and unlocking the striking are located on the left side of the clock between the horizontal portions of the cross shaped supports. The square-sectioned arbor which carries the hammer runs between the horizontal portions of the cross shaped supports on the right. On a clock with a single weight, these positions are reversed.

Exteriors

Now that we have dealt with all the moving parts of the lantern clock we will consider the attractive exterior. For the collector or lover of lantern clocks, the appearance will be in most cases what gives him the desire to purchase. The 'look' of the clock, the dial with the hands, can in particular tell us a lot so let us now proceed to give it our attention.

The early English lantern clock has a dial which can be distinguished as follows:

1. A narrow chapter ring about 2 cm (1 in) wide; on the inside edge will be the divisions for the quarters, i.e. four to each hour;
2. This chapter ring comes completely between the upper and lower plates and is sometimes slightly flattened at top and bottom;
3. Almost always single-handed as a quarter of an hour was sufficient for those days;
4. Often possesses an alarm and therefore an alarm setting disc in front of the dial;
5. Inside the chapter ring there is usually very fine engraving while the corners outside are also very finely engraved; the signature or inscription of the maker is often worked into the engraving at the inner side at the top of the central portion; the style of the engraving is important, indicating the period when the clock was made and a signature engraved on the fret is a sign of an early clock;
6. The hand of the clock is of iron or mild steel and it is an important feature for dating.

Above the clock is a gallery protecting the bell and known as a 'fret'. The fret on the front is engraved, but the side frets above the doors are like the front one in design but have no engraving. Frets come in great variety (see Figs 2–10). It is dangerous to date a clock from its frets. Certainly, in some cases, the maker put his signature on the bottom edge of the fret, but the difficulty is that these decorations are very easy to change. On the other hand, especially on early clocks, there are heraldic motifs and it is wrong to consider every lantern clock with a heraldic fret an early one. Naturally, the best starting point is the signature of the maker; from this we get a much more precise date.

The dial is held in the frame by means of two lugs at the base, which go into holes in the bottom plate. It is held at the top by two pins which are inserted in the top plate in front of the dial. Sometimes, but very rarely, the dial is fire gilt. More often there is a silvered chapter ring and a silvered alarm setting disc. One authority mentions solid silver chapter rings, but I have never seen one. What one often finds, however, is that the dial, doors and columns have been lacquered. This is usually because of the rapid discolouration of the brass. However well it is polished, brass loses its 'golden' appearance in a few days if it is not lacquered. There are good modern lacquers for metal, but formerly a lacquer was used that gave a golden appearance. In fact this lacquer is still obtainable, but it has the disadvantage that the colour darkens in course of time. Some kinds of old lacquer are also hard to remove, which is something of a handicap when cleaning and re-polishing.

Fig. 2   Frets, mainly from 17th century lantern clocks. (After Cescinsky and Webster).

Fig. 3   Frets from some more 17th century clocks. (After Cescinsky and Webster).

Fig. 4 Frets from 17th century lantern clocks. The two lower
ones are from Britten.

Fig. 5   Very common frets. The two lower ones are also seen on French lantern clocks.

[28]

*Fig. 6   Frets of curved design all based on the same
theme. Some features differ.*

Fig. 7   Fret from a 'Sheepshead' (top). The two lower examples are from lantern clocks made for the Turkish market.

Fig. 8   Frets for decorating wings (top) with three frets that are found on small lantern clocks (below). The bottom example is typical for clocks by Joseph Knibb and Christopher Gould.

Fig. 9   Some French frets from small lantern clocks.

*Fig. 10   Two French frets from large lantern clocks (top).
Four examples from small French clocks, mostly alarms
(bottom).*

[33]

Fig. 11   Examples of hands from 17th century clocks.

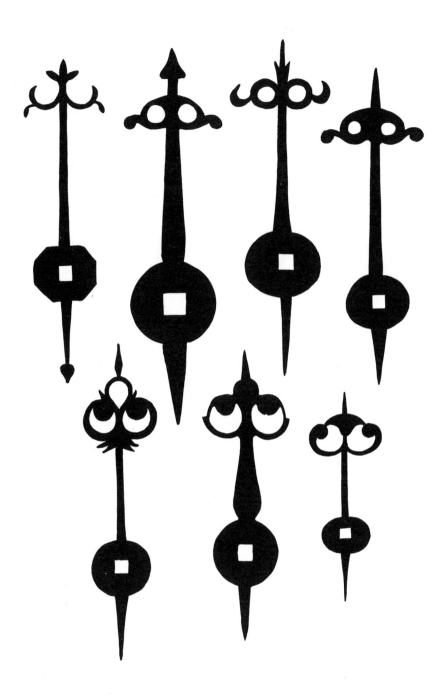

Fig. 12   Hands from 17th century and early 18th century clocks.

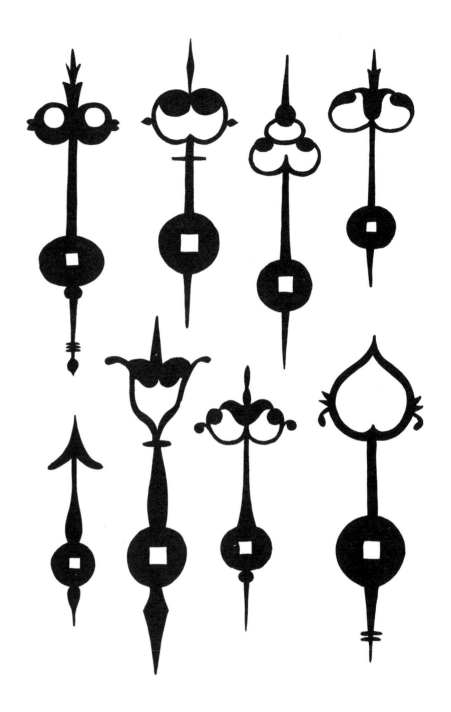

Fig. 13   Hands from 17th century and early 18th century clocks.

[36]

Fig. 14   Hands from 18th century lanterns. In the centre of the bottom row is a pair of hands from a two-handed alarm clock.

[37]

Whilst discussing the colour of brass, it is worth pointing out that antique brass is more yellow in colour than that obtainable today. The brass founders of the past used other proportions for the alloy than are used now. Old brass cannot possibly be compared with, for example, the half-hard turned brass that is usually sold. It is very important for any restorer of lantern clocks to use brass of the correct colour. When replacing doors, or a missing finial or other part, only brass of the correct colour will do. Let me stress that it is no use employing modern brass for restoration; the colour is 'redder' than would be accepted by the average layman. A restorer would do well to acquire antique utilitarian objects of little value as a source of the necessary material for restoration and repair of such things as lantern clocks.

A 17th century lantern clock seldom possesses an oak box for transporting itself and its weights and yet the 17th century traveller was usually compelled to take his own clock with him. Clocks were rare and expensive and for a long time were not present in inns. Thus if any traveller wished to be awakened on time the only solution was to supply his own clock. Also since travelling by stagecoach was always uncomfortable, one did not undertake such journeys willingly. Thus, as the lantern clock was essentially a domestic clock, such very heavy cases have, in the course of time, disappeared—usually by being burned.

3 Types & Variations

Looking now at the different types of lantern clock, we can trace the development from the earliest models to the late 18th century from the following criteria:

1. There are fewer of the lantern type as the manufacturing dates of clocks progress;
2. Chapter rings become larger and broader;
3. Most frames are lighter in construction;
4. Later clocks often have two hands.

While the early 17th century lantern clock had its chapter ring completely within the top and bottom plate, on the later models the chapter ring is cut away at top and bottom to let it come between the plates. Somewhat later, the chapter ring was made still larger and allowed to stick out beyond the top and bottom plates of the frame. To achieve this, a segment was sawn off the fret to make everything fit. This is downright mutilation. The so-called 'Sheepshead' clock has a large chapter ring which sticks out beyond the frame on all sides and therefore hides it.* To our way of thinking this is serious deterioration. A good view of the supporting feet is an attraction and the narrow chapter ring with large central space for decorative engraving and signature are typical features which we are unwilling to give up for the sake of legibility. Admittedly, we have many modern legible clocks but in the 18th century that was otherwise—and a lantern clock should remain a lantern clock!

Sizes

As it is not possible to cite the dimension of each lantern clock illustrated in the book, it is necessary to say something about the size of these clocks.

---

*F. J. Britten, *Old Clocks and Watches and their Makers* (6th edn) p. 532.

The average size of a 17th century lantern clock (if we can in fact talk about an average) is about 41 cm (16 in) total height, i.e. from the bottom of the feet to the top of the finial. The breadth measured over the square portions of the columns is about 16 cm (6 in) while the diameter of the chapter ring is about 17 cm (7 in). These are the dimensions of clocks where the chapter ring is completely between the top and bottom plates, without any cutting away. Very rarely, larger sizes are seen up to a total height of 45 cm (17–18 in). Examples between 25 and 30 cm (10–12 in) total height are very rare, while real miniature lantern clocks are smaller than 22 to 23 cm (9 in). The latter, being very rare are highly prized.

It is important to make the distinction between the complete small clock and the clocks without striking mechanism (the alarms). Complete small clocks are very much rarer than alarms. Alarms with real lantern dials are rarer than alarms with arched dials. The plate to which the chapter ring is fastened is usually engraved and favourite designs were the Tudor rose and the tulip, in various positions. The quality of the engraving does not follow any set rules. There are real masterpieces of engraving and also out-and-out examples of apprentice work, though even these are not unattractive.

One can see a lot of difference in the depth of the engraved work. This can be attributed to the training of the engravers or the orders of the clockmaker. For example, some engraved noticeably deeper and, therefore, broader lines than others and one sees extremely fine engraving or tighter and heavier decorations which look much better when seen from a distance.

Many lantern clocks have their inscriptions placed inside the chapter ring, under the numerals X to II. Signatures in the lower part of the space are also seen, while as previously mentioned they can also be found at the base of the fret.

On later clocks, with broad chapter rings, we see the signature engraved directly on the chapter ring and then between the numerals VII, VI and V. Clocks with arched dials have an ideal place for the signature on a convex plate placed in the arch. However, there are a number of good lantern clocks without any inscription at all.

Clocks with arched dials usually have less engraving. The chapter ring and signature plate are then surrounded by decorative, sometimes gilded, castings, the so-called spandrels. The space inside the chapter ring is then often matted. This forms a 'sandy' surface that is produced by special punches. The technique is difficult, as all parts of the surface must be treated equally.

The work can also be done by etching, and this is identifiable when it is inspected through a glass.

Models

We began with the earliest form of lantern clock. On examination of many of them it becomes clear that even in the early models there is some difference in the proportions of these clocks. We see tall slender lanterns and also short and broad ones. In Chapter 2 it was pointed out that after these early forms, the dial also underwent changes in the course of the years. There are also more interesting variations to be noted.

Lantern clocks were made—and it was undoubtedly the fantastic brainwave of some unknown maker—whereby the pendulum swings between the going and striking trains. These clocks do not possess the usual middle support, but each train in this type has two supports. Between the rear support of the going train and the front one of the striking is a space of about 1.5 cm ($\frac{1}{2}$ in). In this space is found the naturally short pendulum. In order to get the pendulum in this position the clock has to be deeper than usual. A casting is often used for the pendulum bob which is in the shape of an anchor which is seen when the clock is going, but a normal bob is also found even if it has to be a little flattened. The result of placing the pendulum in this position is that the doors must have openings to give the pendulum a clear path. In its simplest form, these are just holes cut in the doors. Then there are doors which possess a triangular pocket with rounded undersides often called 'dog kennels'. The most spectacular, however, are doors provided with 'wings', and these wings give this type of lantern clock its name 'wing lantern' or 'wing clock'. The wings consist of extensions in the shape of a segment of a circle fastened to the appropriate door by means of lips and tapered pins. The wings are surmounted by a special fret that has a purely decorative function. At the front of the wing is a glass so that we can see the pendulum swinging. The inner side of the rear of the wing is often covered with red lead so that it forms a pleasing contrast to the brass.

Wing clocks are rare, especially when they have their original doors, but lost doors are often replaced. It is a pity if this needs doing, but if the work is well done it can be permitted. Look out though for internally soldered wings; they are always false. The good wing is a riveted construction with lips and tapered pins or fitted to the door with screws. The frets are mostly fitted to the upper edge with brass screws and the dials of wing clocks correspond to those of the ordinary ones. Wing lantern clocks with arch dials can also be seen.

Another rare type of lantern is the model where the pendulum comes behind the movement, but inside the frame. With this type, the clock is somewhat deeper than the clock where the pendulum is behind the rear plate. The doors have to have a definite opening to let the pendulum bob come through.

[41]

Another rarity is the lantern clock with quarter strike. These were made by building in a separate quarter train and such clocks with two striking trains are naturally deeper than clocks with only one. A small bell is placed under the larger one for the quarter mechanism and it is fixed to a separate holder fastened to the top plate of the clock. Another variation is the lantern clock with music on eight bells. This plays one scale at the quarters (one blow on each of the eight bells), two scales at the half-hour, three at three-quarters and on the hour plays a fairly long tune, after which the hour is sounded in full on the large bell.

There is a great difference in appearance in clocks made for the Turkish market (Plates 76–79). These clocks, which mostly have an arched dial, are provided with chapter rings having Turkish numerals. The spandrels and doors have been adapted in that we often see the half moon motif. It is remarkable that clockmakers are known to have worked more or less entirely for the Turkish market. Some well known names are George Prior (1782–1822) and Markwick Markham (about 1725–1805). Both these makers made richly decorated bracket clocks as well as lantern clocks for the Turks.

In summarising the special lantern clock variations, there are one or two extra points which should be mentioned. Firstly there is the clock that has two (original) winding holes in the lower part of the dial. In these holes we see the winding squares which operate a many leaved pinion and wind a cord on to a barrel as on long case clocks. Such clocks have, therefore, two driving weights and slots in the bottom plates instead of holes. Clocks of this type are only known from two makers to date, George Harris of Fritwell (1614–94)* and Thomas Ford.† It is noteworthy that the latter made his clock with two hands.

I emphatically stated 'original winding holes'. In the Victorian period, lanterns were made with two winding holes but these are fitted with plate movements driven by springs, which are sometimes placed in the frames of old lantern clocks. Plate movements are those where the trains are contained between two rectangular plates. Sometimes the whole clock dates from this later period. They are simply bad commercial imitations. These clocks which are no longer hanging clocks but purely and simply mantel clocks do not rank for consideration here. I feel that they are simply rubbish.

In the realm of unusual lantern clocks must be included the one by George Newton dated 1660. This clock has no special strike or chime work, but shows the date and the phase of the moon. This is done by

---

Antiquarian Horology (1969) **6**, 5, p. 274.
†This maker is not listed by C. H. Baillie in *Watchmakers and Clockmakers of the World*.

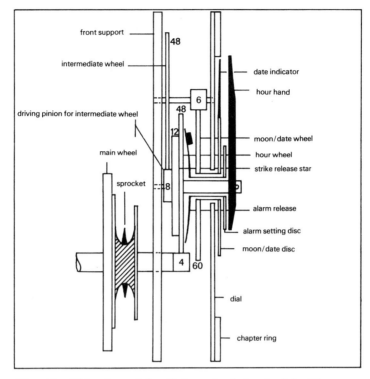

Fig. 15   Side view of the dial work of the clock by Newton.

extending the dial work in an unusual way which is shown in Fig. 15. The earliest English long case clocks which were mentioned in Chapter 2, and provided with lantern movements, have square dials. Sometimes these dials are decorated only with engraving, although one finds dials with cast corner ornaments or spandrels.

In order to get the movement into the case, these movements often lack their turned feet, and sometimes also the finials. Mostly they possess no frets because these would be hidden by the hood of the case.* These lantern clocks have in their original form a verge escapement with short pendulum. Sometimes they have a fret mounted above the square dial.

Escapements

The earliest lanterns have always a verge escapement with a vertical scapewheel and a heavy wheel-balance as regulator. This system, in its original form, is extremely rare. After the application of the pendulum as a result of the invention of Christiaan Huygens (on Christmas Day 1656), we find lanterns constructed with a verge escapement and short

---

Antiquarian Horology (1970), **6**, 8, p. 486 et seq.

pendulum. Huygens did not immediately make his idea public. He first made a number of experiments before he spoke about it, in the first instance, to French scientists.* The time of the introduction of the pendulum into England is also not certain. It is possible that the earliest lanterns fitted with short pendulum can be dated about 1660. We therefore date the earliest clocks that were actually made with a short pendulum as after about 1660.

The invention of the anchor escapement, possibly by Dr Robert Hooke (1635–1703) caused an upheaval in clockmaking. William Clement (CC 1677, mCC 1694–1699) possibly used this escapement for the first time in 1676. The anchor escapement increased the accuracy of clockwork by a very great amount so that after 1676 we find lanterns provided with this escapement and long pendulum. One often sees lanterns on the market which have been rebuilt to anchor escapement. Sometimes it is a clock that formerly had a wheel balance and sometimes one that had a short pendulum. The accuracy of the anchor escapement is such that it is worth the trouble of installing a minute hand. If you find one-handed lanterns with anchor escapement and long pendulum, then they are often rebuilt clocks.

---

*R. Plomp (1972) 'The Dutch Origin of the French pendulum clock' *Antiquarian Horology* 8, 1, p. 24 et seq.

4 Smaller Lantern Clocks

A clock is not valued because of how hard it works but because of how accurately it shows the time

Vauvenargues

As well as the large models of lantern clocks we also find smaller varieties. The reason for the existence of small models must lie in the possibility that they were lighter and took up less room when travelling.

As was mentioned earlier, the lantern clock housed in an inch thick oaken box was often taken on journeys. The clock, complete with weights, was a somewhat heavy object. Although they were carried in a coach there was an incentive to produce them in a lighter form. As pointed out earlier, the 17th century traveller who wanted to be on time had to provide his own alarm clock, for the average innkeeper could not afford one.

The important function of these clocks was to tell the time and wake the owner when required. Striking work in this instance is of secondary importance. Consequently, most of the smaller lanterns were made without striking work. As a result of these smaller and lighter clocks, the driving weight needs to be only half that in a striking clock. There are small lanterns with striking, but they are very much in the minority compared with alarms.

These alarms were called in England 'Timepiece Alarms' (also written 'Alarum'), 'Bedchamber Alarms' or in short 'Alarm Clock'. By 'Timepiece' is meant simply the going work and of course the dial work. If there is an alarm it was called a 'Timepiece Alarm' and in the strict English sense there is no mention of clock. These attractive small lantern clocks have the alarm work always placed inside. This is in contrast to the large lanterns where we find almost always that the alarm is placed outside the iron back plate. Placing the alarm work here is probably the result of lack of space. On large French lantern clocks we see a middle course solution—the alarm work is placed on the outer side of the rear support of the striking train. These alarm movements stick out half way through the back plate (Plate 121). Small French lanterns

[45]

have their alarm work wholly inside the frame as do their English counterparts.

As an original box is rarely found for a large travelling lantern clock, it might be inferred that many such boxes would be found for the small ones. This is not so. Original boxes are very rare, possibly because they had been burnt in after years when the clock had finished its duties connected with travelling. Small lantern clocks are sometimes found in very charming small wall cases. These wall clocks, called 'Hooded Clocks', are known from several eminent makers such as Thomas Tompion (1638–1713) and Joseph Knibb (CC 1670) and also from lesser known makers. In some cases the lantern clock is complete with its frets, simply hanging on a hook screwed into the rear of the case. Sometimes it also stands on a shelf as in a long case clock. The arched dial plate or the rectangular movement plate is often found in hooded clocks.

The small lantern clock has become a sought after object not only by the collector but also by people who want a single good antique wall clock. It does not take up much room, is very decorative and if in good condition is a good timekeeper. It is not considered a clock for fantastic precision and the most important reasons for purchase are investment and attractive appearance.

The latter is also true for certain varietes of the small lantern clock.

Variations

Possibly as a result of orders placed by wealthy people in the 18th century, alarm clocks were made which differed greatly from the accepted pattern.

It is assumed that members of the then reigning houses had these clocks made and took them with them on their travels. One favours this argument because many of the clocks bear the names of famous makers such as Graham (Stender Collection, Antique Fair Delft 1975), Ellicott, Delander and Lindsay (Clockmaker to George III), while less famous names show that also the so-called lesser gods were in a position to deliver a quality product (Blanchard, Atkins, Pepys).

These clocks hung either in the bedchamber of a prince or in the bedchamber of the servant who had to wake him. The clocks were made to order and are much finer in finish than the simpler lanterns.

Such models are a little smaller than the normal small lantern alarms and the characteristic frame of the lantern model has disappeared. The clock by Atkins (Plate 112) is made as a covered-in plate movement while the Lindsay clock (Plates 102–106) has a lantern type frame but with plain square columns. The arbors and wheels are, however, carried between good broad plates. The fine doors of the Lindsay clock are not doors in the strict meaning of the word; they do not open. They have become plates that enclose the sides, with pins which fit into the holes in the bottom plate and are held by a clasp at the top. Their function is decorative as well as protective. The clock has one hand and the chapter ring gives an accuracy of a quarter of an hour which is usual for these clocks. This typical travelling clock has provision for the pendulum to be fastened when travelling. A movable plate with a slot for the pendulum rod holds the pendulum when it is moved down at 90° to the rear plate. A spring fastened to this plate parallel to its length takes care that the pendulum cannot come out of its groove. A similar clock to this is seen in Plate 107, signed William Allam, London. This splendid clock has remained housed in its original mahogany case. The outward difference from the Lindsay clock is that the space inside the chapter ring is engraved while on the Lindsay clock it is matted.

Still another type of travelling clock is seen in the examples by Atkins, Blanchard and Pepys (Plates 108–113). These clocks have a somewhat curved arched front plate that is at the same time a door. The wheels are between plates that at the same time, by means of grooves cut in them, hold the sliding protecting plates at the sides. These plates can only be opened when the front door is opened because there is a strip of brass fastened to this door at the top that holds the side plates when the door is shut. On the left hand plate of the clock by Pepys is the inscription 'Rev P. Le Marsis, Winchester, 1792'. The clock that was apparently made much earlier was, following this inscription, given to the clergyman in 1792.

The front doors have a circular opening so as to allow the chapter ring to be seen, while a glass is fitted for protection. The upper end gives space for the maker's signature while on the lower side the place of origin is stated. Both inscriptions are decorated. At the rear of these clocks we also see provision for holding the pendulum; the well known partly opened eye that is familiar on bracket clocks.

An even simpler arrangement is found in the clock by Arlander Dobson, London (Plate 114). This clock is a pure timepiece. It possesses only a going train and dial work. The form of the door is also different; the arch is not in a double curve and the front is not opened as in the previously described clocks but it slides upwards, for which purpose a knob is fastened to the rear of the arch.

French Lantern Clocks

For purposes of comparison it is worth looking briefly at a few French models. The French made lantern clocks in very different form from the English ones. In general, they are more lightly constructed and possess their own character. Quite often there are completely different features such as an intermediate strike for the half-hours. The French also built various models of lantern clock—the large examples, 'normal', and also small ones. They never made wing clocks, however, although I recently saw a French lantern where the pendulum was between the going and striking trains. This clock had never had doors and therefore no wings either.

Plate 1 Lantern clock inscribed 'John Holloway att Lavington fecit' made entirely of iron and dated 1611. The six-sided columns are unusual and only the chapter ring is of brass.

[49]

Plate 2   Rear view of the Holloway clock seen from above. The balance, with its decorated spoke, is clearly visible.

Plate 3   Detail of the Holloway clock with the signature on the bottom of the fret; note the very narrow chapter ring.

[50]

Plate 4   A balance clock seen from above. The large single armed balance is mostly cast brass, but iron ones are known.

Plate 5   A very unusual clock, with indication of date and moonphase, signed 'Georges Newton 1660' on the shield within the fret.

Plate 6   A close-up of the dial of the Newton clock.

[53]

Plate 7   A close up of the splendid signed fret of the Newton clock shown in Plate 5.

Plate 8a   Detail of the hand of the clock shown in Plate 8b.

Plate 8b   This balance clock is inscribed at the base of the front fret with the words 'William Sellwood at ye Mermayde in Lothbury' (CC 1633–1652). Lothbury is a street in London. The hand of this (shown in Plate 8a) clock is very unusual in that the straight ends were made especially prominent in order to facilitate setting with the thumb and index finger. The inscription on the fret is typical of an early clockmaking practice.

Plate 9 An archetypal example of a fine 17th century lantern clock. The completely open hand is peculiar to this type and the inscription reads 'William Bowyer of London fecit' (1626–1647).

Plate 10 Another particularly fine lantern clock with a balance by 'William Bowyer in Ledenhall Street fecit'. Note the fine engraving inside the chapter ring which fills the available space in a very graceful manner.

[57]

William Bowyer in Ledenhall Street fecit

Plate 11   A close up of the Bowyer dial shown in Plate 10.

Plate 13   A close up of the engraved fret with the dolphin motif on a clock by Thomas Knifton.

Plate 14   Detail of the inscription on the bottom of the fret of the same Knifton clock. The engraver, here not at his best, cut 'Lothbirry' instead of Lothbury! It is not uncommon for differences also to occur in style and spelling of the makers' names e.g. Closson and Closon.

[60]

Plate 15   A special presentation clock by 'Ahaseurus Fromanteel Londini fecit'. The master's signature is in a drapery above the figure VI. This balance clock is dated around 1632–1656.

Plate 16   A lantern clock with balance and unusual spherical supports to the feet. Unfortunately, this early 17th century clock is unsigned.

Plate 17   An early clock by 'Peter Closon near Holborne Bridge Fecit'.

Plate 18 A simple lantern by Peter Closon, without any chimes or even an alarm.

Plate 19 A clock with quarter striking inscribed 'Peter Closson Neere Holburne Bridge Londini fecit'. (CC 1636–1653). This early clock already has two hands and minute and quarter-hour indication on the outside of the chapter ring.

*Plate 20   Another clock with quarter-
hour striking but with a different fret
inscribed 'Peter Closon Londini fecit'.
The balance is clearly visible behind
the gallery.*

*Plate 21   The same Closon clock seen from the front with dial, fret
and large bell removed.*

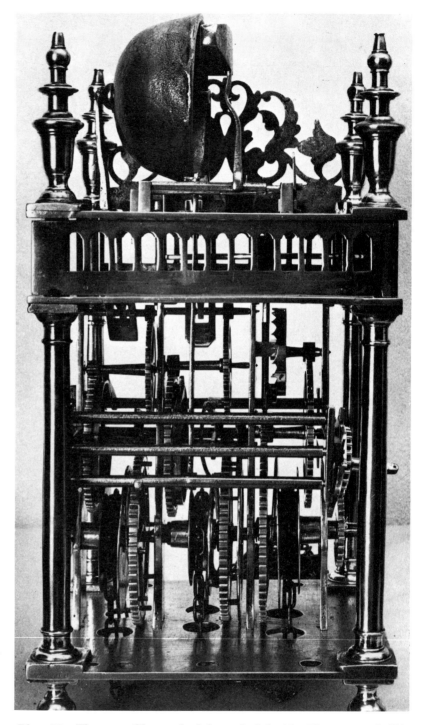

Plate 22   The same Closon clock from the left side. The quarter bell is mounted under the large bell.

Plate 23   A remarkable clock inscribed 'Thomas Ford de Bucks fecit'. This early clock is two-handed and is shown without its bell holder and bell. Note the original winding holes.

Plate 24   An unsigned 17th century balance lantern clock.

Plate 25   This same clock has a special feature in that the hammer arbor is placed between two separate plates.

[71]

Plate 26 A lantern by Nicholas Coxeter made 'Neer Gold Smith Hall'. This clock was probably made to order on account of the inscription at the bottom of the fret. It may have been a wedding present.

Plate 27   The dial and chapter ring of the clock by Coxeter. The space in the centre, which is normally covered by the alarm setting disc, has been used as a trial piece by the engraver. Here he also inscribed the date 1665.

Plate 28 A balance clock with an unusual chapter ring by 'Nicholas Coxeter at ye 3 Chaires in Lothbury Londini fecit' (CC1646, mCC 1671–1677, died 1679).

Plate 29   A balance lantern inscribed 'Jonathan Chambers fecit' (c. 1690). It is interesting that the dial carries only the signature and possesses no further engraving.

[75]

Plate 30 A very fine engraved lantern clock with a double top plate. The balance is set between the two top plates and can be seen through the gallery. The signature reads, Richard Beck at ye French Church' (CC 1653–1658).

Plate 31 A very great rarity—a clock with the pendulum at the front. This was normal for clocks originating in central Europe (the so-called cow-tail pendulum) but very rare in lantern clocks.

Plate 32   A close-up of the pendulum mounting of the clock in the previous illustration. Note the very rare fret with the 'Lion and the Unicorn' design.

Plate 33   A clock engraved 'Thomas Trafford fecit'; (London c. 1665).

[79]

Plate 34   A somewhat broader lantern clock by 'John Ebsworth at ye Crosskeys in Lothbury Londini fecit' (CC 1665, mCC 1697–1703).

Plate 35   Close-up of the engraving inside the chapter ring on the Ebsworth clock.

Plate 36   An engraved door of the Ebsworth clock. According to the style of the engraving and the way the surfaces are filled, the doors appear to be later than the clock.

Plate 37 A lantern inscribed 'Edward Webb of Chewstoke fecit 1681'. The 'Lion and Unicorn' fret is rare. The placing of the signature and date in the corners of the dial is also very unusual.

[83]

Plate 38 *A clock of about 1640 by Samuel Turner with a movement with verge escapement and wheel balance. Note the extra tall finials, above and below, which are made in one piece with the columns.*

Plate 39   A lantern clock by Robert Robinson, London (CC 1652–1656) with verge escapement and wheel balance.

Plate 40 A clock by William Hol-loway of Stroud (1697–1723) with the number 92 and very fine heavy columns. The chapter ring is some-what broad and slightly flattened at top and bottom.

Plate 41   Lantern clock by Richard Rayment St Edmundsbury of about 1740. The chapter ring is flattened at the top, while at the bottom it penetrates the base plate.

[87]

Plate 42 A lantern made in Scotland. The decoration is less classical that that of its London contemporaries. In addition the columns are thinner and less graceful in contour while the engraving is poorer.

[88]

Plate 43   A clock by 'William Dobson in High Holborne fecit' (1670–1684). The pendulum swings inside the case of the clock; the doors have holes to let the pendulum through.

Plate 44   The same type of clock from Langley Bradley, London (CC 1695). The pendulum in this clock also swings inside the case.

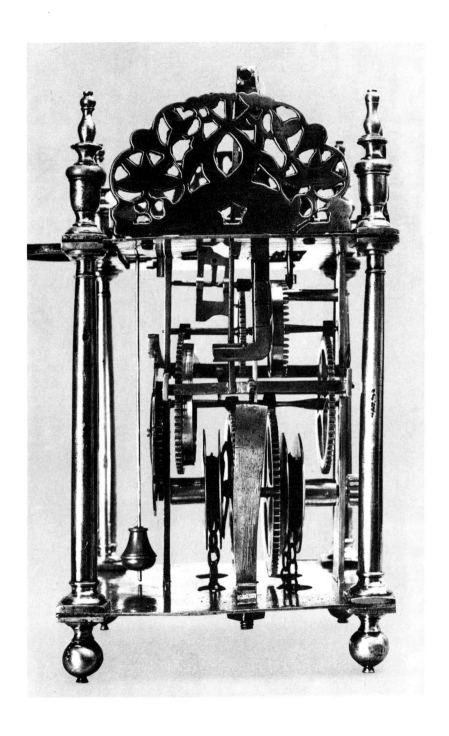

Plate 45 Side view of a lantern clock where the pendulum swings inside the frame.

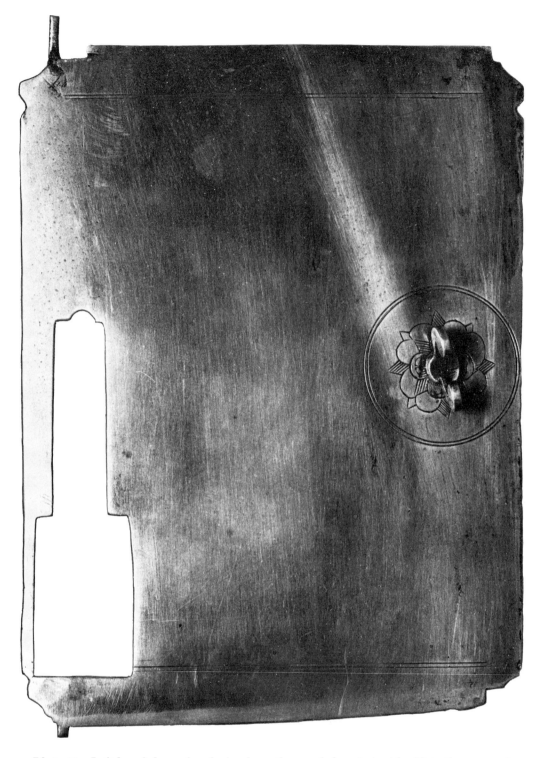

Plate 46   Left-hand door of a clock where the pendulum is inside. Note the engraving around the hasp.

Plate 47   Lantern clock by Edward Hemins of Bister (Bicester) who died in 1744.

[93]

Plate 48   A simple lantern clock by William London.

Plate 49 A lantern clock by John Disborrow of Ashen of about 1700.

Plate 50   A lantern clock by William Webb of Taunton.

Plate 51   A lantern clock by James Drury, London (CC 1694, mCC 1728).

[97]

*Plate 52   A clock by James Malden at
Rayne in Essex about 1740.*

*Plate 53   A real 'Sheepshead'; the frame is almost entirely hidden.
The base of the fret fits the chapter ring.*

Plate 54   Side view of a lantern clock with musical work.

[100]

Plate 55   A wing lantern clock by an anonymous maker.

[101]

Plate 56   Lantern clock with wings by John Ebsworth (CC 1665, mCC 1697–1703).

Plate 57   Wing lantern clock engraved 'William Speakman in Hatton Garden fecit' (CC 1661, mCC 1701–1717).

Plate 58 Wing lantern clock, by 'William Barlow, Lynn Regis'
(Lyme Regis); second half of the 18th century.

Plate 59   An anonymous wing lantern clock. Note the decorative outline of the feet.

Plate 60   A wing lantern by an anonymous maker from the second half of the 18th century.

*Plate 61   A wing lantern clock with an arch dial by James Vines of London (about 1708).
The straight lines of the dial are broken by the wings making this a very attractive clock.*

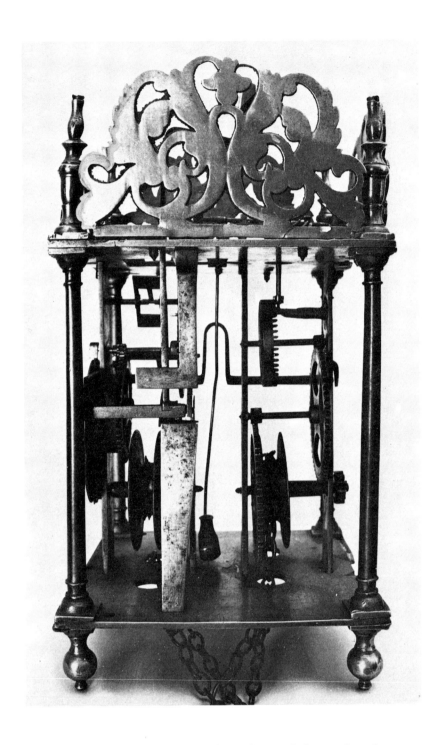

*Plate 62   Side view of a clock where the pendulum swings between
the going and striking trains. Here the pendulum bob is a flattened
knob. On wing clocks one usually finds an anchor-shaped bob.*

Plate 63   Detail of the fret on a wing.

Plate 64   Detail of the anchor shaped pendulum bob of a wing clock.

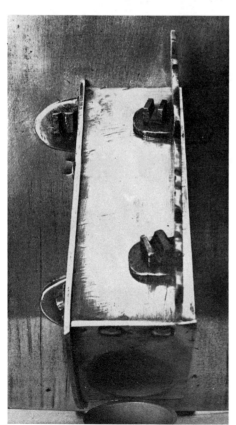

Plate 65   Detailed side view of a wing.

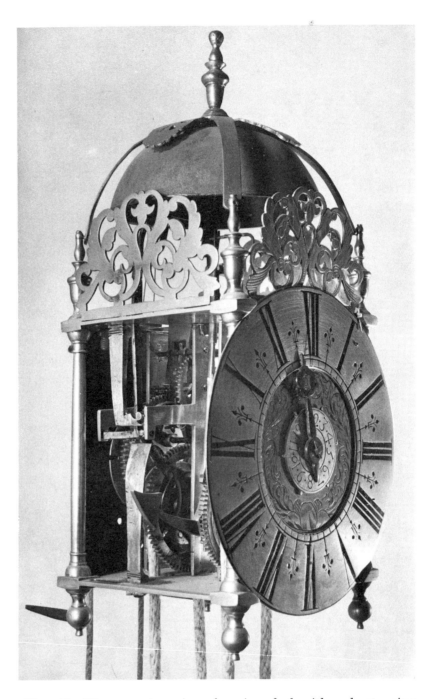

Plate 66   Three quarters view of a wing clock with a chapter ring which is much too big; the feet are partly filed away. From the second half of the 18th century.

Plate 67 Alarm setting disc from a
17th century lantern clock.

Plate 67b Another alarm setting
disc from a 17th century lantern clock.

Plate 67c Alarm setting disc from an
18th century lantern clock.

Plate 68   A view from below a lantern clock where the going period has been increased by driving with a pulley.

Plate 69   Rear view of a lantern clock. The alarm work is mounted on the iron back plate.

Plate 70   A large bell with bearers and finial.

Plate 71   The decorated bell bearers seen from above when actually mounted on the clock.

Plate 72   *A decorated bell bearer c.f. Plate 71.*

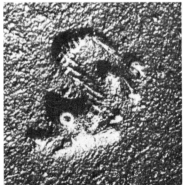

Plate 73   *A caster's mark in a bell—in this case a small dragon.*

[115]

*Plate 74   Close-up of the dial engraving of a clock by 'Gulielmus Cother: de Covent Garden'
(about 1668). It is remarkable in that the signature does not read 'William Cother of Covent
Garden' so possibly it was made for a French customer.*

Plate 75   Close up of the dial engraving of the clock in Plate 50.

Plate 76 A lantern clock for the Turkish market made by William Burton of London (1744–1770). The later alarm setting disc strikes a discordant note.

[118]

Plate 77   Side view of another clock made for the Turkish market with an unusual fret.

Plate 78 Another side view of the Turkish lantern clock. The half moon motif is quite common on this type.

Plate 79　A beautifully engraved door of a lantern clock also made for
Turkey. The fairly open style of engraving indicates a date in the
second half of the 18th century.

*Plate 80   A smaller model with an
unusual fret.*

Plate 81   Another small balance lantern inscribed 'John Greenhill, Ashforde fecit' and in a fine state of preservation for such an early clock.

Plate 82 Another small lantern clock engraved 'Andrew Savery Londini fecit' (1676–1693). This clock is a timepiece-alarm.

Plate 83 An early small lantern inscribed 'John Ebsworth Londini fecit.' (CC 1665, mCC 1697–1703). This splendid clock, with its narrow chapter ring and filed down feet, formerly had wings. The movement was found with only the going train intact. All the striking work and the alarm were lost. The fine front fully justifies the restoration work.

Plate 84 A small lantern clock from none less than Joseph Knibb of London, (1640–1711, CC 1670). This clock is noteworthy for the fact that it has two hands.

Plate 85   A small lantern clock by Charles Goode of London (about 1686). The minute hand is a later addition, as can be seen by the punch marks on the outside edge of the chapter ring.

Plate 86 Movement of a hooded clock by 'Peter Closon London fecit'. Unfortunately the case is lost.

Plate 87   Side view of clock shown in Plate 86.

Plate 88   The verge escapement of a small lantern clock seen from above. The verge has the so-called book pallets.

Plate 89   A so-called hooded clock by Richard Jarrat of London, (CC 1670, mCC 1685–1695).

[130]

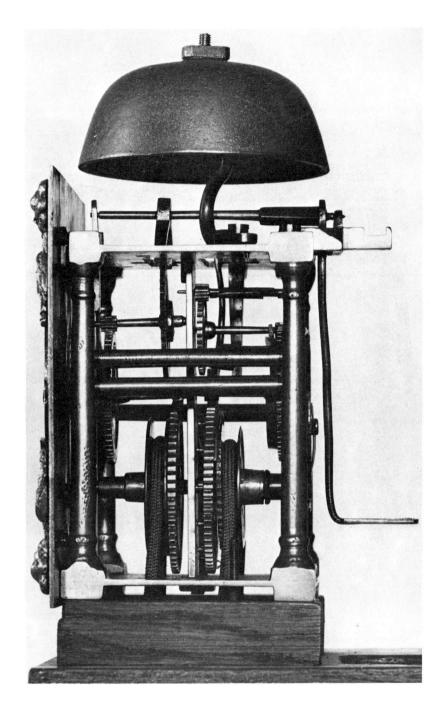

Plate 90   Side view of the movement of the hooded clock by Jarrat.

Plate 91   A 'Timepiece' (going train only) in a small case. A hooded clock by Richard Peckover of London, numbered 519. From the first half of the 18th century.

Plate 92   An unsigned lantern clock with an engraved dial in place of spandrels.

*Plate 93   Small arch dial alarm lantern by Daniel Quare of London
(born 1649, CC 1671, mCC 1708, died 1724). The hand appears to be a
later addition.*

Plate 94   Side view of a clock by John Watts of Canterbury.

Plate 95 Full view of the same lantern alarm by John Watts.

Plate 96   Alarm clock by Samuel Denton of Oxford. From the second half of the 18th century.

[137]

Plate 97   A two-handed alarm by Hamley of London (1775–1840).

Plate 98   Another Denton clock from Oxford.

Plate 99   Alarm clock by George Wren of London from the second half of the 18th century. This clock already has two hands.

Plate 100   Alarm clock by Panchaud and Cumming of Oxford Street, London (1799–1824).

Plate 101   Small alarm clock signed by John Page, London. The engraved doors are not at all common.

Plate 102   An almost identical clock without a case by George Lindsay, London (1776). Lindsay was clockmaker to George III.

Plate 103   Rear of the Lindsay clock shown in
Plate 102. The pendulum is free.

Plate 104   Rear of the Lindsay clock with the
pendulum fixed.

Plate 105   Side view of the Lindsay clock.

Plate 106 Side door of the Lindsay clock open.

[145]

Plate 107   A great rarity. A very luxurious travelling clock in its original mahogany case by William Allam of London (CC 1743–1785).

Plate 108   A travelling alarm by John Pepys of London (CC 1680, mCC 1707–1715).

Plate 109   A side view of the Pepys clock with the inscription.

[147]

Plate 110   Rear view of the Pepys clock.

Plate 111   Door of the Pepys clock open, clearly showing the alarm work.

[148]

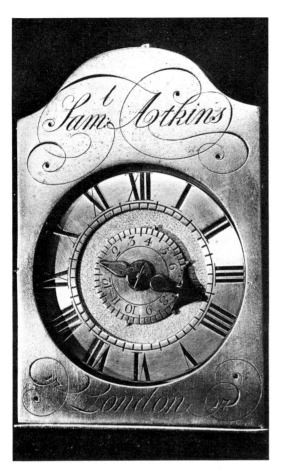

Plate 112   Identical clock by Samuel At-
kins of London (1697–1768). The hand on
this clock is not original.

Plate 113   Identical alarm clock by Charles
Blanchard of London (1688–1768).

Plate 114   A timepiece by Arlander Dob-
son of London (1772).

Plate 115   Side view of the Dobson clock.

[150]

Plate 116 A small French lantern clock with going, striking and alarm work by Pierre Le Roy à Meaux. In 1686 this maker went as a refugee to Amsterdam.

Plate 117 A simple but pleasing French lantern clock. Each part is marked with a crowned 'R' (see detail on Plate 118).

Plate 118 On some French lantern clocks there are punched-in makers' marks—here a crowned 'R' on every part of the clock.

[152]

Plate 119   A French lantern by Des Hayes of Abbéville. The clock has an iron frame and differs greatly from what one usually finds in English lantern clocks.

Plate 120   Close-up of the fret of the clock by Des Hayes in Plate 119.

Plate 121   At the rear of the Des Hayes is the alarm mechanism half built into the plate and held by a bridge.

Plate 122 With the bell removed the three hammers are visible; one is for the single stroke at the half hour, then comes the large, thick hammer for the hour strike and at the rear the normal, double-sided alarm hammer.

Plate 123 The half-hour strike is arranged by raising the hammer with a twelve pointed star.

Plate 124   A French lantern of the 'Sheepshead' model with a typical French dial, a so-called 'Twelve Piece'. The cast fret is crowned with the French cockerel. Note the double portrait of Louis XIV, under the figure XII and under the pedestal on which the cock stands.

Plate 125   A French alarm of the 'Sheepshead' model. Only the feet of the frame can be seen. The fret is broadened and runs with the curve of the chapter ring. Made by Le Doux of Paris in the first half of the 18th century.

Plate 126   A small French alarm lantern
clock by Francois Le Begue of Paris. It has
a specifically French fret. The bell hangs
from a simple support and there are no side
frets. From the first half of the 18th century.

Plate 127   The Le Begue clock seen from
the side. Note the fastening of the bell
support.